ENCOURAGEMENT

FOR *Today*

BY

Noah Washington

Watersprings
PUBLISHING

ENCOURAGEMENT FOR TODAY
Published by
Watersprings Media House, LLC.
P.O. Box 1284
Olive Branch, MS 38654
www.waterspringsmedia.com

Contact publisher for bulk orders and permission requests.

ISBN 13: 978-1-948877-83-1

Dedication

I dedicate this devotional first and foremost to **God**, to whom I spent time with for the production of this book.

Second, I dedicate this book to my wife **Twila** who gave me time and space to work on what God has given me. She's the real MVP.

Last, I dedicate this book to my son, **Noah Alexander** and my daughter **Drew Mackenzie** who love me endlessly and whose maturity allows me to do what I do. Thanks guys for being two great kids.

Introduction

Many of us have often been encouraged to "read the Bible". At this point in my life, I certainly know the value of and power in sitting down to read the Bible, meditate on God's word, and use those words as guidance for my life, my thoughts, and my deeds. But I also understand that simply suggesting someone read the Bible is less effective, especially if they are new in their relationship with God. The Bible is a big deal and can sometimes feel overwhelming and out of reach.

When I thought of writing Encouragement for Today, I did so with a desire to help those individuals who don't regularly read the Bible. Whether it is because they don't fully understand or know how to interact with it yet or they just haven't fully committed to the practice doesn't matter to me. What matters is that they have access to a supplement that helps them to better understand the Bible. This devotional is that supplement. I like to think of it as a companion, a bridge of sorts that can help them walk closer and closer to the Word of God.

So, wherever you might be in your journey, I hope you receive encouragement from God's promises and that this devotional will allow you to look at His promises in a way that is unique and meaningful to you. If you're just starting to form a relationship with God; if you are working towards building, growing, and sustaining your relationship; and even if you've been here and done this before, this devotional is for you.

Use this guide in the morning, evening, or at any other time in which you feel the urge to work on your link to God. Commit to making it a part of your day. Refer to it often. Use the reflection questions as an avenue to a deeper, more thoughtful connection with yourself and God.

Ultimately, my prayer is that you will find this book at just the right time for your life...a time during which you can hear and understand what God is saying specifically to you. I pray that you will be encouraged, today and every day.

Day 1-

Psalm 13:1-2
"How long, Lord? Will you forget me forever? How long will you hide your face from me? How long must I wrestle with my thoughts and day after day have sorrow in my heart? How long will my enemy triumph over me?"

It doesn't matter who you are or what your status in life is… these questions always seem to haunt us. Waiting on God to do what you've asked Him to do and even what His word says He will do, is so hard especially when nothing in your life seems to resemble His promises for your life.

Don't try and make up a plan because your made-up plan will never equate to God's will. After you have cried, screamed, and fought through pain…remember that Godly waiting is never wasted time but is always worthy time.

My encouragement for you today is to understand, though difficult, that God's timing is perfect, and in His will is the best place for you to be.

Be blessed!

Reflection Questions

1. What causes the most confusion and frustration for you in life right now?

---

2. Do you believe that you are in the center of God's will?

---

3. What do you normally find brings the most stress in your life? Why?

---

4. What do you believe to be God's plan for your life?

Day 2-

Psalm 139:14
"I praise you because I am fearfully and wonderfully
made, your works are wonderful, I know that full well."

I t's interesting how much we have changed God's design for our lives. Even though our creation came at the hands of God, we have recreated ourselves into an image that God never intended for us to be.

Many of us cannot praise God because of our own recreation. God cannot get His due praise out of our lives because our recreation is constantly fighting against His creation. We allow people, places and things to mold our change and we wake up one morning and don't even realize who we are anymore, which is a child of God. I am so thankful that His word declares that if anyone is in Christ He is a new creation!

My encouragement for you today is to allow
Christ to inform you of who you are and reject
whatever pushes you away from what you were
created to be.

Be blessed!

Reflection Questions

1. Who has God created you to be?

_____

_____

_____

_____

2. Do you regularly thank God for how He has created you? If not, why?

_____

_____

_____

_____

3. What gifts has God placed inside of you that you are not using to your full potential?

_____

_____

_____

_____

4. What does God want you to do based on what He has placed inside of you?

_____

_____

_____

_____

Day 3-

John 14:27
"Peace I leave with you, my peace I give to you. I do
not give to you as the world gives. Do not let your
hearts be troubled and do not be afraid."

Stress is not of God! It doesn't come from God nor should God be given credit for it. God gives peace...peace so that your human heart will not be troubled or forever feel dis-ease. I don't know who is going through a stressful moment today, but if you are, please know that feeling stressed just means that you are human but giving power to stress may mean that you are unfamiliar with Gods power.

We stress out because we feel that regardless of what we have heard, read, or seen, we sense that God does not know what He is doing, or He may be a bit confused about our situation. We stress because for some reason we feel that in stressing about it we can find a remedy for it. However, there is only one remedy for a stressful heart, and that is a peace-filled heart, only obtained through Jesus Christ. If God promised you peace, then believe it.

My encouragement for you today is to look
stress right in the eye and repeat a Godly
promise.

Be blessed!

Reflection Questions

1. Do you trust God with all of your heart? If not, why?

_____

_____

_____

_____

_____

2. What consumes your mind for the majority of the day?

_____

_____

_____

_____

_____

3. What or who do you normally turn to when you are stressed out?

_____

_____

_____

_____

_____

4. Do your coping techniques cause more harm to you?

_____

_____

_____

_____

Day 4-

Psalm 46:1
"God is our refuge and strength, an ever-present help
in trouble."

Don't act like you have never needed help before! One of the challenges of the Christian walk is that we are often filled with so much pride that we will seldom admit to the fact that we are desperately in need of serious help and assistance. Many of us would even place more energy into convincing people of what we aren't rather than asking God on a daily basis for help in becoming who we need to be. While some would admit to being in need of help it does not usually translate into the amount of time spent asking God and pleading with God for the help we know we stand in need of. Do we honestly want Godly help, or do we simply want to be relieved of something that is bothering us? When the power of God comes to help us it's not just coming to lift a burden, it's also coming to change our attitude. Help is not just coming to fix a problem, but also coming to tell us no. Why use and trust your power, which is limited when you have access to Godly help, and power which is limitless?

My encouragement for you today is to
acknowledge the awesome power of God and
the help that is at your disposal RIGHT NOW!

Be blessed!

Reflection Questions

1. Are you usually too proud to ask for help when you are in trouble?

_____

_____

_____

_____

2. What kind of trouble has presented itself to you in the last year?

_____

_____

_____

_____

3. When you are in trouble do you often feel as if it's your fault? Why?

_____

_____

_____

_____

4. Do you believe that God is trustworthy?

_____

_____

_____

_____

Day 5-

Psalm 91:1
"Whoever dwells in the shelter of the Most High God
will rest in the shadow of the Almighty."

Wouldn't it be wonderful to be aware of the thoughts and plans that God has for your life? Wouldn't it be great to know where you are supposed to be, what career you are supposed to be in, or who God has reserved for you to be in a marital relationship with? Don't you get frustrated with pressing through life thinking your way through and wishing that whatever you are doing God is involved in it. I am learning that God often withholds information from you because He knows that you are not close enough to Him for you to keep the secrets He shares! David shares that power comes from living in a secret place with God! Because we don't often immerse ourselves in that place, God withholds from us certain details about our life. Let's be honest, we are more like visitors and guests in the secret place than we are residents and regular attendees.

God is not slow. He knows that we often want the blessings more than the ONE who alone can give those blessings. Don't become that person who God knows as the person who enjoys gifts more than the gift-giver!

My encouragement for you today is to find
yourself in that place with God not simply to get
information but to understand who God is.

Be blessed!

Reflection Questions

1. Do you believe you have gotten to the place where you feel like you have a strong relationship with God? Why or Why not?

_____

_____

_____

_____

2. Paint a picture with words about what you desire your relationship with God to look like.

_____

_____

_____

_____

3. What currently gives you the most excitement in life?

_____

_____

_____

_____

4. What is keeping you from having a powerful relationship with God?

_____

_____

_____

_____

Day 6-

Matthew 19:21
"Jesus answered, 'If you want to be perfect, go and sell
your possessions and give to the poor, and you will
have treasure in heaven; Then come, follow Me.' "

I have been there-where I want God to make everything smooth with no problems. I've gone through too much already and honestly don't feel as though I have any more in me to push through. I feel that based on everything I've already experienced I shouldn't have to push anymore. Why can't God just make everything easier? Why can't God simply open all the doors and separate the Red Seas for me? Wouldn't it be easy for Him to exercise His power on my behalf? Don't you feel that sometimes you deserve a blessing? You've put your time in as a Christian and it's time for you to get something in return. However, that is not what it means to follow Jesus. What annoys me often is the fact that following Jesus includes difficulty, struggle, and sacrifice. In true Christianity there is no wealth without work, there is no victory without defeat, and there is no joy without pain.

Following Jesus does not mean that He has told you exactly where to go, but it does mean that He is leading you. Which also means that whenever you're following Jesus, He's not too far away!

My encouragement for you today is to
understand that the beauty of following Jesus
is...in following Him!

Be blessed!

Reflection Questions

1. What is the most difficult thing about following Jesus?

2. Where do you sense the Lord is leading you right now?

3. Why are you afraid to fully follow Jesus right now?

4. What needs to happen in order for you to follow Jesus?

Day 7-

Psalm 18:29
"With your help I can advance against a troop; with my
God I can scale a wall."

I t is apparent to me that I honestly don't really know the power that God has! The Lord God can cause me to leap over walls, His power is proven and is a shield! And yet, I spend so much time trying to substitute God's power for other things: a job, relationships, television, social media, and the list can go on and on. There is no test that God needs to go through to prove that He can do what He claims He can do...He's proven! Even though He is proven, Malachi records that God says you can put Him to the test. God is so humble that He will ask you to test Him on something that He doesn't need testing on. Have you ever felt that regardless of what God has done before, you always want or need God to prove Himself once again?? For some reason, we always hold God on trial in our minds and the only way He gets off is if He does exactly what we want Him to do. However, God does not need to perform more for you to establish Him as God. God will always be God and God will always have power. His ways are perfect, and His power can cause you to leap over walls!

My encouragement for you today is to look for
Gods power in your life and thank Him for how
His power has impacted your life.

Be blessed!

Reflection Questions

1. What has substituted God's power in your life? What have you practically replaced God's power with?

_____

_____

_____

_____

2. Why do I make God pass certain tests in my mind?

_____

_____

_____

_____

3. List five things that have happened in your life that you know for a fact it was God who did it.

_____

_____

_____

_____

_____

4. Have you honestly thanked God for the ways He has performed in your life?

_____

_____

_____

_____

_____

Day 8-

John 2:9-11
"And the master of the banquet tasted the water that had been turned into wine. He did not realize where it had come from, though the servants who had drawn the water knew. Then he called the bridegroom aside and said, 'Everyone brings out the choice wine first and then the cheaper wine after the guests have had too much to drink; but you have saved the best till now.' What Jesus did here in Cana of Galilee was the first of the signs through which He revealed His glory; and His disciples believed in Him."

Have you ever wondered when the situation in your life was going to change or if your condition was so bad that nobody could turn it around? If you are like me, what is often frustrating is wondering if and how God is going to turn your problems into praise. For many of you, you feel like its been bad for so long that maybe you will forever have a 'watered-down' life. But the Bible says that Jesus can turn your water into wine. He can turn water into wine. He can take whatever is boring, uneventful, problem-filled, or difficult and turn it into something beautiful. Regardless of how bad it is Jesus can turn the tears in your eyes into a beautiful smile. Jesus can turn the depression in your heart into dancing in your feet. Don't wallow where you are and be held back to never experience the change. Change is coming!

My encouragement for you today is to allow God to change you.

Be blessed!

Reflection Questions

1. If you had the power, what would you change in your life right now? Why?

_____

_____

_____

_____

2. Are there some habits and issues in your life that need to be changed? What are they?

_____

_____

_____

_____

3. What miracles are you waiting for God to perform in your life?

_____

_____

_____

_____

4. How can you partner with the power of God for these miracles to take place?

_____

_____

_____

_____

Day 9-

1 Corinthians 10:13
"No temptation has overtaken you except what is common to mankind. And God is faithful; He will not let you be tempted beyond what you can bear. But when you are tempted, he will also provide a way so that you can endure it."

God's faithfulness in your life is not just seen in providing for your needs and giving protection, but God's faithfulness also shows up during your temptations. Have you ever wondered why some of the negative things that you have wanted to do never happened? It's because God's faithfulness was greater than your power to do wrong. This doesn't simply manifest itself with illicit sex, drugs, or bad music. His faithfulness has shown up in places where you wanted to speak evil back to someone or say words to people that you would later regret. Not only is God's faithfulness great, but His trust in you is great! He believes that whatever comes your way does so because you are strong enough, through His Spirit, to overcome it. He isn't just faithful, but He has faith in me. Faith in me to stand up against any temptation that comes my way.

Smile, knowing how much confidence God has in you. Smile, knowing how much faith God has in you, to know that you are much stronger than you think, and you can stand in the face of temptation. You don't have to say yes to the enemy. Just smile knowing that a big God thinks a lot about you.

My encouragement for you today is to smile!

Be blessed!

Reflection Questions

1. What are some of the biggest temptations that you currently deal with?

_____

_____

_____

_____

2. What trials are you facing in life right now?

_____

_____

_____

_____

3. How has God's faithfulness been seen in your temptations and trials?

_____

_____

_____

_____

_____

4. How have you grown spiritually through your temptations and trials?

_____

_____

_____

_____

_____

Day 10-

Galatians 6:9
"Let us not become weary in doing good, for at the proper time we will reap a harvest if we do not give up."

Have you ever felt like living for God isn't getting you anywhere? You attend church, pray, read, and strive to live for God and yet it seems that things are just not happening the way you want them to. In fact, you are so frustrated with praying the same prayer that you wonder why God hasn't come through on that prayer already, after all, He must know what you need—especially since you've been saying the SAME thing to Him. Waiting on God can sometimes feel as if nothing you are doing means anything and everything you are doing is accomplishing absolutely nothing. Are you there right now? Do you honestly want to forget everything and go live on a deserted island to live out the rest of your days where you won't have to worry about waiting, wanting, or worrying? The Bible teaches us that although it's difficult, if we keep pressing and don't give up—living for God has its own rewards. When you live for God you are sowing seeds that will reap a harvest in your life. When you stop living for God, you block your own blessings. We don't live for God to be blessed; however, blessings are a bi-product of obedience! Each day we live for Him, we are sowing seeds that in the right season will reap a harvest! What will that harvest look like though? Keep living for Him.

My encouragement for you today is to keep living for God—DON'T STOP!

Be blessed!

Reflection Questions

1. What are you waiting for God to do in your life right now?

_____

_____

_____

_____

2. What does it mean to live for God?

_____

_____

_____

_____

3. What results did you expect to happen in your life by now that aren't being seen?

_____

_____

_____

_____

4. List five promises in scripture that encourage you to hold on to God.

_____

_____

_____

_____

Day 11-

Psalm 32:8
"I will instruct you and teach you in the way you
should go; I will counsel you with my loving eye on
you."

*Y*ou're confused, aren't you? You have no idea where you are supposed to be, or where you are supposed to go. Which job you should take, or which position to be in is something unfamiliar to you. Or perhaps, you simply feel confused about where you are and why things are happening the way they are. This is not simply a season where God is choosing to withhold some information from you or has you in a time of waiting. You are mostly confused and unsure because you have neglected to tap into the ONE person who can let you know exactly what needs to be known for where you find yourself. David tells us that God will teach us the way we should go, and God will instruct us and advise us! If then you are unsure it could be that you have not spent enough time listening to God or being patient enough with God for Him to reveal to you what you are unclear about. What better person to teach you about His way then God Himself! I am amazed at how many voices I allow dominate space in my mind daily. Often, I let those competing voices dominate so much so that God isn't given the opportunity to teach, guide and direct me. Be open for what God desires to tell you...it could change your entire life.

My encouragement for you today is to stop
allowing everybody else give you instructions
except God.

Be blessed!

Reflection Questions

1. Why is it so easy to trust yourself?

2. Do you feel that your way is best, or is it difficult to talk to God about what you should do?

3. Who or what do you turn to most often for advice or direction?

4. How can you practice trusting in God for direction?

Day 12-

Isaiah 43:2
"When you pass through the waters, I will be with you;
and when you pass through the rivers, they will not
sweep over you. When you walk through the fire, you
will not be burned."

Have you ever felt overwhelmed before? No, I mean like literally, incredibly overcome with everything that you have going on in life. You may even be at the point where it's so much going on that you can't even talk about everything. It's a lot isn't it? School, work, family, bills, unemployment, relationships, your job, grief, sickness, sadness, loneliness, pain, disappointment...it's way too much. And usually when you are going through all these things you don't know many people who can identify with all of your pain. Don't give up hope today. The Lord tells us that whenever we pass through waters He is present with us. When we pass through rivers, those rivers will not sweep over us. When we walk through the fire, we won't be burned. This tells me that even though I experience what looks to be something that overwhelms me, God is there. Not only is God there with you, but if you think those things you are going through are going to destroy you—they're not! If you think that all those things you are experiencing are going to kill you—they're not! Whenever and wherever you are going through, God is right there, and wherever the Lord is there is liberty! At the place where you thought you were going to die, you will thrive and survive.

My encouragement for you today is to know God
is with you when you walk through fire.

Be blessed!

Reflection Questions

1. Are you overwhelmed with life right now? If so, why?

2. Do you feel as though what overwhelms you is larger than God's power?

3. Is the knowledge of God being with you enough to comfort you?

4. Write down instances in your life where you know that God was with you.

Day 13-

Psalm 34:18
"The Lord is close to the brokenhearted and saves
those who are crushed in spirit."

There are times in life when people and situations simply let you down, and you are left with the misfortunate situation of being the only one who feels the pain from it. Has this ever been your place in life? Where your heart literally aches because it has been broken. A breakup, a breakdown, some unexpected devastating, terrible news...all can bring you to a place where your heart is broken. Not only that, but you will agree with me that oftentimes these situations don't always bring us to our knees but sometimes they take us further away from God and our spirit begins to be crushed.

Are you there right now? If so, how long has it been since you have honestly connected with God? David says that the Lord is close to people who have a broken heart and a crushed spirit. The more broken you are, the closer God is!

No matter how hard it is, keep pressing through to make sure no matter how someone or something has hurt you, that you tell God all about it, after all—He is extremely close to you because of how hurt your heart is. Whenever your heart is broken, He's never far away!

My encouragement for you today is to always
keep the lines of communication open between
you and God.

Be blessed!

Reflection Questions

1. What things in your life have broken or crushed your spirit?

_____

_____

_____

_____

2. Do you normally see God working through your pain, or do you usually see your pain without God working?

_____

_____

_____

_____

3. Do you feel that the people who have hurt you have caused you to distrust God?

_____

_____

_____

_____

4. How do you best communicate with God? How would you rate your communication with God: Solid, Occasional, Weak? Why?

_____

_____

_____

_____

Day 14-

Proverbs 14:29
"Whoever is patient has great understanding, but he
who is quick-tempered displays folly."

Anger is not just lashing out in terrible fits of rage at other people, but anger can also be termed as the negative disposition that you have against other people. What you think about others is revealed by how you act and react towards them. Did you know that your attitude can actually cause great misunderstandings in your life? Meaning, you can be filled with so many negative feelings that it causes you spiritual blockage in receiving what you need from God. And what I am learning is that many of us catch an attitude or hold on to our negative dispositions. But may I suggest that maybe so much of your decision-making has been off because of your attitude problem? Your problem is not that you don't read the Bible, pray, or even serve in ministry...it's that while doing all of this, you do it with an attitude.

Look for ways that you can share the love of God with someone and be genuine about it. When you do get upset with someone and say things that are offensive and demeaning—apologize. Your attitude could be holding up your spiritual progress.

My encouragement for you today is to literally be
nice to people.

Be blessed!

Reflection Questions

1. Do you struggle with controlling your anger, or does your anger manifest itself in different ways?

2. Do you find yourself at times taking your anger or attitude out on other people?

3. What usually makes your attitude adjust daily?

4. Is it difficult for you to be nice to people?

Day 15 -

Romans 8:26
"In the same way, the Spirit helps us in our weakness.
We do not know what we ought to pray for, but the
Spirit Himself intercedes for us through wordless
groans."

Have you ever felt like you weren't getting your prayers through, or that your prayers weren't effective? Sometimes life is so difficult that it seems as though the words of prayer that come out of your mouth fall straight to the ground. At other times you may feel so overwhelmed that you don't even know what to say to God. In certain seasons of your life you may even feel as though what you pray doesn't even matter and that you aren't worthy to receive what you are asking the Lord for.

Let me first encourage you by saying that your words do not impress God. God does not get excited when He sees that you are using new words when you pray, nor does He raise His eyebrows in shock when we seem to be praying for a long period of time. However, the Bible teaches us that because we don't even know how to pray or know what to say when we pray, the Spirit of God helps us. God helps us pray to Himself! And this is how He helps us—The Spirit of God prays for us that what we say to God might have power. Are you kidding me?? Stop trying to impress God with words and impress Him with just wanting to talk to Him regularly. That's what excites God—when we spend time with Him on a regular basis.

My encouragement for you when you pray is to
stop trying to be so deep.

Be blessed!

Reflection Questions

1. How would you rate your prayer life: Solid, Occasional, Weak? Why?

2. Do you struggle with spending time with God in prayer?

3. What do you find yourself praying about most often?

4. Did you grow up in a home that taught the value and power in prayer?

Day 16-

Psalm 103:12
"As far as the east is from the west, so far has He
removed our transgressions from us."

Sometimes you can get so overwhelmed by your sin. When you think back over your life and what you did, who you were with, the people you hurt, and the time you wasted doing things that didn't produce the best results—it can be extremely overwhelming. At the time, you didn't really think about the results of what your decisions would cause. You did not account for how your future would be affected by past behavior, and it can leave you just sitting in your room with your eyes filled with tears wishing and wanting to just turn the clock back to the time when your sin drastically impacted your life. However, you now just feel overcome with feelings of guilt, sadness and even depression. Not only because of your own decisions but also the enemy will at these times make you feel unworthy as if you aren't good enough. Haven't you been there before? When the enemy just made you feel worthless? However, this will make you smile—The Bible says that as far as the east is from the west is the distance that God removes my sin from me! Don't let the devil make you think that your present won't be blessed because of your past. If you have repented, God has removed your sin from you!

My encouragement for you today is to not allow
your past sins to keep you from experiencing
your present reality.

Be blessed!

Reflection Questions

1. Do you think a lot about stuff you have done in the past and how much it has impacted your present or future?

_____

_____

_____

_____

2. Are you frequently discouraged because of where you are based on the decisions you have made?

_____

_____

_____

_____

3. Do you struggle with believing that you are forgiven?

_____

_____

_____

_____

_____

4. How much of your past is impacting the productivity of your present?

_____

_____

_____

_____

_____

Day 17-

Philippians 4:13
"I can do all things through Him who gives me strength."

I get extremely tired sometimes. I mean like times when I don't want to get out of the bed or I just want to stay at home all day. Life can oftentimes bring you to a place of fatigue where every bit of your energy feels taken, drained and it can seem as if no vitamin in the world will help. Life can sometimes make you feel as if you can't do anything, and the enemy will prey on what life already does and he will make you feel as if you don't have the capability to do anything. If you haven't experienced it yet, there will be times in your life where you mentally feel like a little baby and it seems as if you don't know anything. You will try to perform duties, and be creative but you are at a loss, you have nothing to give. I've been there, haven't you? When I am there I get so down on myself because I feel like I don't have it together...I get frustrated at myself because the creativity is gone, the intelligence has seemed to fade, and all of my strength is gone. And in these times, I literally feel like giving up. But I am so glad that God promises me that I can literally do anything, all things...whatever, because its Christ who will give me the strength to do it. This also means that it's quite possible that I have been relying on myself way too much. Furthermore, as a practice, realize that anything good that comes out of my life happens because Christ gave me the strength to do it. Put everything on Him, because He is built to handle it, not you!

My encouragement for you today is to trust the power of Jesus Christ in your life.

Be blessed!

Reflection Questions

1. Do you feel that you are accomplishing things in life, or do you feel that you are just spinning your wheels going nowhere?

_____

_____

_____

_____

2. So far, what have you accomplished this calendar year?

_____

_____

_____

_____

3. Do you possibly have more confidence in yourself than you do in God?

_____

_____

_____

_____

_____

4. When are you going to begin trusting God to help you accomplish things?

_____

_____

_____

_____

_____

Day 18-

Isaiah 40:31
"They that wait on the Lord will renew their strength;
they shall mount up on wings as eagles; they shall run
and not grow weary, they will walk and not faint."

No part of waiting is fun. There is nothing exciting whatsoever about it. In fact, if anything, it becomes more and more annoying the more that you wait. You will agree with me that waiting for anything can often be one of the most frustrating things that you have ever done. The tough reality though is that waiting is not only part of life, but for believers waiting is something that strengthens our relationship with God. To strengthen our relationship with God, and to appreciate Him more—we wait. The wonderful thing about God though is that waiting on Him is never wasted time.

When you are waiting for God to do what He promised He will not only give you back the strength that you exhausted, but you will also begin doing things you've never done before. God will make good on every promise He has ever made, which means that when the waiting is over you will have spiritual power like never before—IF you truly wait. Some complain the entire time, try and work it out themselves, or try and convince God why they are worthy of receiving now what they are waiting for. But when you wait on God, you will have strength like never before!

My encouragement for you today is to get
excited while you wait.

Be blessed!

Reflection Questions

1. What are three things that you believe God has promised you that you are waiting to receive?

_____

_____

_____

2. While you are waiting for God, what are you normally found doing?

_____

_____

_____

3. What do you waste most of your time doing?

_____

_____

_____

_____

4. What are three things that have happened in your life that have helped to grow your faith?

_____

_____

_____

_____

Day 19-

Proverbs 13:20
"Whoever walks with the wise becomes wise, but the companion of fools will suffer harm."

Who is in your company and who do you spend a lot of time with? Not simply hanging out with, but texting, calling or messaging. The company that you keep, to a large degree can literally spell out your spirituality. The Bible teaches us that iron sharpens iron, which means that one of the reasons that many of us continue to lead dull lives may have much to do with the people who we associate ourselves with. One of the reasons that we will stay in toxic relationships is because we may feel a sense of loyalty or devotion toward the individual. There are even some instances where we will justify the dysfunction of our relationships based on our need to be loyal—even when the relationship leads us to go against God's word. Take stock and inventory of your relationships because you may find your relationship with the Lord has stalled because of your relationships with other people. Ask yourself these questions:

1. Do I find myself compromising God's word because of the relationship?

2. Does the relationship pull me away from God?

3. Has this relationship been a great source of encouragement?

My encouragement for you today is to take stock
of every single relationship and analyze how it
affects your relationship with God.

Be blessed!

Reflection Questions

1. What are some characteristics and qualities of the company you usually keep?

2. Do your friends push you to become better or to be complacent in mediocrity? How have they pushed you and how have they kept you stagnant?

3. Do you find yourself compromising God's word to stay in certain relationships?

4. Do your relationships pull you away from God?

Day 20-

Proverbs 22:24-25
"Do not make friends with a hot-tempered person, do
not associate with one easily angered. Or you may
learn their ways and get yourself ensnared."

It can often appear that people who care nothing about us seem to care a lot about what is happening in our lives. This is why it is extremely important to stay close to the Spirit of God, because he can reveal to us everything we need to know. Without the Spirit of God, we end up giving an audience to people who we believe have our best interests at heart and yet they only want from us what makes them feel good. Usually individuals who are takers, come off as givers; and people who are givers sometimes can feel like takers in the beginning.

We then wake up one morning and realize that we have gotten deeply involved with people who carry things that aren't often easy to get rid of. How many times have you entangled with people who seemed to be worth millions only to find out that you could have gotten them off of a discount rack. Some people have a spirit of anger that is so strong that once you connect with them, it takes years to get that spirit out of your system. Not only is it hard to disconnect once you have connected but the Bible says that once you entangle yourself with a person like that you begin to copy their ways.

My encouragement for you today is to make
sure you are connected to the Lord.

Be blessed!

Reflection Questions

1. Are there a lot of people who take from your life but don't pour back into your life?

_____

....

....

....

2. Are you connected to so many people, places, and things that it is difficult for you to connect with the Lord?

_____

....

....

....

3. Are you confident and comfortable with the people you are allowing into your space and your spirit?

_____

....

....

....

....

4. How much room do you have that is honestly reserved for God?

....

_____

....

....

....

Day 21 -

Psalm 138:7
"Though I walk in the midst of trouble, you preserve
my life."

How can my life have meaning even when it appears that what is going on right now is so meaningless. How can there be productivity from my life when the product that is currently being presented is an extremely shallow one. Please understand that it is frustrating to find some sense of meaning, worth and significance when it seems as though everything happening in your life is troubling.

Have you ever been in a season in life where it feels as though absolutely nothing is going right? You may be in that season right now! What I love about God is that even though it seems my life is out of control He promises that He will preserve my life. This promise should encourage you today because it is a reminder that anything good that comes out of your life is not based on you, but He takes personal responsibility to ensure that your life will be kept intact. If this were the case, we would be depressed daily. But look at what the Lord promises. He promises that even in the middle of trouble He will maintain your life. God's got you, so...

My encouragement for you today is to stop
measuring success and failure in life based on
what you do or don't do.

Be blessed!

Reflection Questions

1. Do you believe that there is a Godly purpose in your life? If so, what is it?

2. Do you often feel that there is no reason to live? Why is that?

3. Is your life's success based on what those around you are doing?

4. How would you describe your life? How do you think God looks at your life?

Day 22-

Romans 12:2
"Do not conform to the pattern of this world, but be transformed by the renewing of your mind. Then you will be able to test and approve what God's will is—His good, pleasing and perfect will."

There are times when I wish that God would just come down and sit right next to me beside my bed and say: This is what will happen in your life in the next year. There are other times when I wish that God would send me a text message, an email, or even a hand-written letter laying out for me everything that I need to know so that there will be no confusion as to what I am supposed to do, where I am supposed to go, or even when everything will happen. But I also know that at times it is incredibly difficult to hear from God sometimes. It's easier for me just to do what seems best to me rather than to be patient and determine what the will of God is for my life. Let me caution you because it almost always seems as though living in the perfect will of God problem-free. It's almost as if we want to live in the will of God so that we can experience a perfect life. However, I would argue that God's perfect will does not guarantee a perfect life. If your mind changes then regardless of the experiences that you face in life you can still have peace, knowing that you are living in God's will. Living in God's will—which can be difficult at times—is better than being absent from God's will and experience no problems.

My encouragement for you today is to allow God to change your mind.

Be blessed!

Reflection Questions

1. What do you understand God's will for your life to be?

_____

_____

_____

_____

2. What have people in your circle told you that you are supposed to be doing with your life?

_____

_____

_____

_____

3. Is your mind open to fully following God's will, regardless of how daring and crazy it may seem?

_____

_____

_____

_____

4. Why is it so easy for you to morph into the patterns of this world?

_____

_____

_____

_____

Day 23-

1 Peter 5:7
"Cast all your anxiety on Him because He cares for
you."

In today's society it is painfully obvious that people have an issue with loving. I mean some people will sometimes show concern for one another, but many people are really just out for themselves. It's a difficult thing when you find yourself seemingly walking through life alone. It's tough when the people who said they would be there for you are nowhere to be found. It's hard because this life seems to throw so many things at us. Every time you look up it can appear as if something else that you did not expect or plan for is being put on you. Have you ever felt as if a cross is being placed on your shoulder, and you are walking through the worst time in your life?

I am eternally grateful though that I have a God who is able to take whatever is on me and place it on Him. Why? Simply because he cares about me! God cares about me so much so, that He will take from me WHATEVER is bothering me. I can place on the Lord EVERYTHING that is causing me fear, worry, or pain! Like really...give it to Him! He cares about you and He doesn't mind taking your stress. We have a God who can be stress-filled and not be stressed!

My encouragement for you today is to give to
God whatever is pressing you down.

Be blessed!

Reflection Questions

1. Are there people in your life who unconditionally care about you?

2. Do you have at least one person in your life who you can talk about your issues in life with and they don't judge you?

3. How often do you get stressed out? What are your life stressors? How do you cope with them?

4. What does it practically mean to cast all of your anxiety on God?

Day 24 -

John 15:7
"If you remain in me, and my words remain in you, ask whatever you wish, and it will be done for you."

One of the things that I love to do is honestly...go home. To go home after a long day and hang out there with family and sometimes friends is an experience beyond compare. Being at home, knowing that it is a place of peace and a place of rest is one of the best things this life has to offer. It brings a sense of joy knowing that you can be in your home and be secure from whatever has happened or is happening on the outside. There are things you immediately have when you are at home: a place to rest or relax, a place to prepare for the next day, and a place to refill yourself from expending too much energy.

Likewise, Jesus says that when we live in Him and His words live in us we automatically receive some things. What better person to get something from than the Lord. He says that when we live in Him and His words live in us we can ask Him whatever we want, AND it will be done! Maybe the reason why I haven't been receiving certain things is because I am living in the wrong house. Where I spiritually live isn't a place that affords me much. It's time for you to pack up where you are living and move to Jesus' house. When you move, there are certain things that you will begin receiving. If you stay in the house where you currently are...you will continue to live in lack.

My encouragement for you today is to move.

Be blessed!

Reflection Questions

1. What and where is your comfort zone in life?

2. What causes you to become uncomfortable?

3. Do you know enough of God's word to know what word you can hold Him to?

4. What prayers have you been praying over the last year that have not been answered?

Day 25-

Proverbs 18:10
"The name of the Lord is a fortified tower, the
righteous run to it and are safe."

This world can oftentimes be an incredibly scary place! Every time I look at the news, there is another tragic accident, killing, or hostile takeover that places everything in perspective for those watching. If that wasn't enough, life also brings stressors that we can't seem to get away from. School work, our jobs, family members, financial distresses...all have a way of bringing some kind of fear over our lives. Life at times is even so difficult that it seems like everywhere you turn, you look into the face of another factor that causes some type of difficulty or fear. Where can we go? What can we look to? Is there even something that can provide some type of relief?

The Bible says the name of the Lord alone is a strong tower. That means that calling on the name of the Lord brings strength. Make no mistake about it, you are going to need some help in this life, and the name of the Lord offers the help that you need. Nothing else will do it quite like the sound of His name will!

My encouragement for you today is to call on the
name of the Lord!

Be blessed!

Reflection Questions

1. What are five of your worst fears and why?

2. Where do you receive the most help from?

3. How often do you call on God for help?

4. Who do you normally call when you need help in life?

Day 26-

1 Corinthians 15:58
"...Let nothing move you. Always give yourselves to the work of the Lord, because you know that your labor in the Lord is not in vain."

Sometimes I feel like moving ahead of God. I feel like He isn't moving fast enough or doing what I feel needs to be done at a particular time. And if I can be real honest, there are even times when I feel that He doesn't even know what He is doing. I know, I know that's a crazy thing to say—but it's true. Based on what I am dealing with I feel like He doesn't really know what He is doing. Because of this, I start trying to fix the situation and handle life by myself.

However, I am challenged by this text today to be steadfast and immovable. I am challenged to stop trying to do so much and simply live in the power of God. Have you ever heard the phrase: "You're doing too much!" That's exactly what God is telling you today. You are spending most of your time trying to remedy what you think you have control of. You are "doing the most" trying to work things out. You are working too hard! The apostle Paul says to abound in the work of the Lord! Trust what He is doing. I know it can be difficult at times since there are times when you think that He doesn't know what He is doing. He never gets tired of doing things for you. Be steadfast in His work and stop doing so much, accomplishing nothing.

My encouragement for you today is that God
never gets tired of working for you.

Be blessed!

Reflection Questions

1. Do you sometimes feel like leaving God because God does not seem to be doing anything on your behalf?

2. How do you stay encouraged to hang in there?

3. What pushes you to quit instead of hanging in there?

4. Does it bother you when you feel that you don't know what God is doing in your life?

Day 27-

Matthew 7:5
"You hypocrite, first take the plank out of your own
eye, and then you will see clearly to remove the speck
from your brother's eye."

I will be the first to admit how easy it is to critique and criticize someone else. It is arguably one of the easiest things to do, and many of us have gotten so good at it that it's almost like breathing to us. I want to suggest however that constantly criticizing or talking about another person—putting other people down is a critical sign of our own dysfunction. We think sometimes that placing people beneath us gives us strength in our minds. However, when we regularly practice this behavior it is actually because of how little we value ourselves. Small minds are limited to the practice of finding things in an individual's character to somehow make them feel better. People who constantly degrade others are blind. They can't see the possibilities in another person, so all they are able to see is the negative character that emanates from them. They are never able to see the greatness inside of another person because they are blind to any reality of greatness. People should never be your measuring stick giving you a picture of where you should be. I encourage you to stop wasting time and energy in the futility of degrading other people. It profits you nothing and in doing this, it tears you down.

My encouragement for you today is to evaluate
where you are more than taking stock of where
other people are.

Be blessed!

Reflection Questions

1. Do you love to gossip?

2. Do you struggle with low self-esteem?

3. Do you often compare yourself with other people?

4. How can you become more confident in who God created you to be?

Day 28-

2 Timothy 1:7
"For the Spirit God gave us does not make us timid,
but gives us power, love and self-discipline."

I wonder how many things would have been accomplished in your life if you weren't scared to do it? How many people in this world would have been blessed if you stepped out and did what was already in you to do. I believe that everyone who is allowed the privilege to be on planet earth has the amazing responsibility to produce what God has already planted inside of them. When God created man, He gave them a command to produce! Productivity is part of your humanity. Non-production is a sure sign that life is slipping away from you. The world is waiting for more people to be productive in their God-given purpose, however most people are scared to do it. Fear is not something that comes from God. God gives us power to be productive and the enemy gives us fear to keep us stagnant. The real question that we all have to ask ourselves is why am I so scared to do what God has already given me power to do? Why are we so fear-filled to be productive in areas that God has already given us the green light and told us that He would bless us? Do what God has given you the power to be productive to do. What are you waiting for? You are not going to fail, God has already given you the power! Don't be overcome by fear...God has given you power, love and the mind to do what He has put in you to do!

My encouragement to you today is....DO IT!

Be blessed!

Reflection Questions

1. What would you do if you were not scared to do it?

2. Why are you so scared to do what God has given you the power to do?

3. What are you waiting for in order to be more productive?

4. Write down what you believe God is calling you to do.

Day 29-

Matthew 6:34
"Therefore, do not worry about tomorrow, for
tomorrow will worry about itself. Each day has enough
trouble of its own."

In a world of confusion and difficulty it is so easy to be stressed. It's almost as if stress has become a normal part of life. We will worry about everything that is behind us, pressing us, and things that have yet to happen that we aren't even sure will happen. If there is one thing that I have come to know and understand about the Lord, is the fact that worry, fear, and stress do not come from God. He is not the author of those feelings. Those are thoughts that come from the enemy to weaken our faith and to break our confidence in God. Have you ever noticed how stress oftentimes pushes you not to pray, seek God, or read His word? It's as if the devil knows that being worried about life will cause us to stay away from God. Stop thinking the worst about your life that hasn't even happened yet. The enemy does not control your destiny. People do not control your future. God is the ONE who has authority over future and destiny! And if God is before you then nobody can touch you! It is the will of God that every single need of yours be supplied. Your future is amazing! Stop believing the lies of the enemy and accept the truth of God's word, that there is no need to worry about what will happen because God has your future in His hands.

My encouragement for you today is to PRESS!

Be blessed!

Reflection Questions

1. Is your stress level pushing you away from private and personal time with God?

_____

_____

_____

_____

2. What are you worrying about that has not happened?

_____

_____

_____

_____

3. Is your stress turning into depression?

_____

_____

_____

_____

4. Is your stress paralyzing you?

_____

_____

_____

_____

Day 30-

Isaiah 35:4
"Say to those with fearful hearts, Be strong, do not fear; your God will come, He will come with vengeance; with divine retribution He will come to save you."

One of my favorite movies of all time is a classic movie called, Rudy. It's about an undersized young man whose lifelong dream was to play college football at Notre Dame. Since his grades were not good enough to immediately enroll he enters Holy Cross to get his grades up and then hopefully get a chance to try out for the team at Notre Dame. While discouraged about where his life was, he talked to a priest at Holy Cross who tells Him this classic line: "After years of studying the Bible, there are only two things that I know to be true—Number one, there is a God; and number two I'm not Him." It bothers me at times when life is not going how I thought it would turn out. Doesn't God know that I don't enjoy what is happening in life right now? One thing I know is that God's Word does not lie. Our problem is having to deal with the timeline of receiving God's word and realizing that God's time is very different from ours. Isaiah tells me that I should be strong and that I should not be afraid because God will come to my rescue! When is it going to happen? I'm not sure. I just know that He is coming.

My encouragement to you today is that regardless of what is making you scared or afraid---don't fear because God is coming to get you out of it!

Be blessed!

ENCOURAGEMENT FOR TODAY

Reflection Questions

1. What are some fears in your life that you have yet to face or address?

_____

_____

_____

_____

2. Explain what you don't enjoy about your life right now.

_____

_____

_____

_____

3. How has God come through for you in the past?

_____

_____

_____

_____

4. Does your frustration in life sometimes come from the fact that you are in control of your life?

_____

_____

_____

_____

Day 31-

Proverbs 29:25
"Fear of man will prove to be a snare, but whoever
trusts in the Lord is kept safe."

This must be said to you today: "STOP PUTTING SO MUCH TRUST IN PEOPLE!" Now I understand the normal need and feeling to trust people who are family and who are close to you. However, it can be extremely frustrating to place so much trust in people and those same people let you down. I am learning that when we place so much trust in people we honestly have no strength and energy to place faith in God. It does take some level of power from us to put faith in people, places, or things. When we have used up our energy to put faith in things that have let us down before when God comes asking us to put our faith in Him we have absolutely nothing to give to God...nothing.

Placing faith in God is an investment in your destiny. When you place faith in other people it oftentimes blesses them more than it blesses you. However, when you place your faith in the Lord you are investing in your future. If being with the Lord for eternity is where you want to spend your future, then placing faith in God is a great place to make your current faith investments. Don't place faith in temporary people for long term results. Instead place faith in the only Person who has stood the test of time.

My encouragement for you today is to give God
the first energy of your faith.

Be blessed!

Reflection Questions

1. Is your current distrust in God linked to how many people have let you down in the past?

2. Are there people who have hurt you in the past that you are honestly not fully healed from?

3. Are you able to pray for the people who have hurt you?

4. How much of your faith have you been giving to people that should be reserved for God?

Day 32-

Zephaniah 3:17
"...He will rejoice over you with singing..."

Most of us would not imagine the Lord singing, much less making up a song about us. God usually gives songs to other people. He oftentimes inspires people to write songs about Him so that other people can be encouraged. There have been many times in my life where my spirit was lifted, and I felt like I could press a little further based on the lyrics of a song that made me feel like God had everything taken care of. There are songs that have even moved me to tears to the point where the tears would not stop flowing because the words of that particular song meant so much to my current experience. However, the Bible says that there are times when God drafts His own songs. And the crazy thing about these songs is the fact that these songs are about YOU? What is it about my life that would cause the Creator of the Universe to write a song about me and then sing that song loudly, and excitedly over my life?? I am in shock and awe that God would even want to write a song about me and then smile while singing it based on the poor behavioral tendencies that I have in my life.

My encouragement to you today is for you to remember that even though people may not celebrate you, the Creator God is writing songs about you...that should make you smile today!

Be blessed!

Reflection Questions

1. How much of what you are doing in life is based on people's expectations of you?

_____

_____

_____

2. Compare and contrast your good and poor qualities.

_____

_____

_____

3. Are the negative words that people have spoken about you, causing you to believe them?

_____

_____

_____

_____

4. Find 10 promises in God's word that tell you what God thinks about you.

_____

_____

_____

_____

_____

Day 33 -

Micah 7:7
"But as for me, I watch in hope for the Lord; I will wait
for the God of my Savior; my God will hear me."

I t is oftentimes difficult to be honest with yourself in your Christian walk with the Lord. For many of you reading this, you don't have spiritual accountability and so it becomes worse to be honest about where you really are and how you are progressing in the Spirit. The truth is, there are so many things that we look to and we hang on to, to help us cope with the difficulties in life. Seldom do we totally wait on God to move before we try to work out things on our own. We don't often struggle in the Spirit, or stay on our knees, or fully look to God with all our issues.

Honestly, we don't fully believe that God will rescue us, and we don't like God's timetable in our lives. Some situations will take you 15 minutes to get into but will take you 15 years to get out of; and it could have been remedied had we waited on the Lord—knowing that He will hear! Don't make future decisions that you don't know much about anyway. Don't be in such a rush to go nowhere.

My encouragement to you today is to stop being
so fast.

Be blessed!

Reflection Questions

1. Who are your accountability partners? Name them.

_____

_____

_____

_____

2. Have your accountability partners proved helpful in your spiritual journey? Why or Why not?

_____

_____

_____

_____

3. Are you making plans for your life without the Lord's leading?

_____

_____

_____

_____

4. What are you in a hurry to complete or do in your life?

_____

_____

_____

_____

Day 34-

2 Peter 3:9
"The Lord is not slow in keeping His promise as some
understand slowness..."

I f there is one thing that I do know about God it is the fact that He does not lie. He always tells the truth...Always! It is part of what makes Him God. It is part of His DNA. God just doesn't lie, and if God happens to make a promise to you, trust and believe that what He promised you will happen. What is often frustrating is dealing with God's timetable in your life. How He works and the timing with which He works can often be disturbing because it has nothing to do with how you feel He should be working. How God works is not subject to you or how you think he should move. His activity is not subject to you; however, it is subject to His promises. You may think that God is moving slow, but when God makes you a promise, the promise is often never tied to a date. God will often give you a promise but not tell you when the promise will come to reality in your life. The only thing that you have to hold on to is His promise. Forcing God into a timetable in your mind diminishes what in fact is coming, which is the fulfillment of His promise! I know it seems like it is taking a long time but know this one thing: God does not lie.

My encouragement for you today is to not hold
God to a timetable.

Be blessed!

Reflection Questions

1. How strong was your relationship with your parents growing up?

2. Has there been a time in your life when you felt that God let you down? Was there something you felt as though God should have done that He did not do?

3. Describe the environment in your home of origin.

4. Do you feel as though your life is out of control, or do you have control of it?

Day 35-

Ecclesiastes 3:11
"He has made everything beautiful in its time..."

We spend much of our lives trying to make ourselves become what we were never created to be. It's almost as if when God was making us He made some critical and crucial mistakes and to help Him out we spend a large portion of our existence trying to become what God never intended for us to be. Because we are not satisfied with God's decisions with us we try to manufacture what we believe God should have done, and we try to do it in quicker time than what we think is taking God too long. One thing that I have discovered about God, is the fact that He takes His time to work on us and work with us. God is not in the business of microwaving you for the kingdom. His desire is not to snap His finger and, in an instant,, make you what He wants you to be. Instead God takes His time with you. And the blessing with God taking His time is that in the process, you develop a relationship with Him and not simply become a better person. He takes His time with you because of His great love for you. He believes in and is invested in what He wants you to be. Don't spend time worrying about how long it takes; just take the time growing more in love with Him.

My encouragement for you today is to be
encouraged by God's timing.

Be blessed!

Reflection Questions

1. Does your life resemble the beauty of God?

2. Does your inward beauty match your outward beauty?

3. What are some things that God is working on in your life? What issues in your character is God dealing with?

4. What is frustrating about what God is working on?

Day 36-

Proverbs 3:5-6
"Trust in the Lord with all your heart and lean not to your own understanding in all your ways submit to Him and he will make your paths straight."

Sometimes our greatest temptations are not sex, music, or any outward thing that many people point to feeling they represent sinful practices. However, sometimes our greatest temptation comes in the form of trust. It's the temptation of whether or not to trust God with everything that we have. It's the question we have to answer of trusting God or trusting the enemy.

You can probably reflect back in your own life of specific instances where you chose to trust the enemy and the outcome was not positive. Leaning to your own understanding or trusting yourself is essentially trusting the enemy. He told Adam and Eve that they would become like God—that they would receive the ability to be able to make decisions on their own without God's input.

That is honestly what gets us in the most trouble and gives us much of our difficulty in life, when we decide that our way is better than God's way. Understand that God knows everything and is willing to share with you things that will radically change your life if you would only ask Him.

My encouragement to you today is to realize that you don't have all the answers.

Be blessed!

Reflection Questions

1. Be honest, do you trust the Lord with all of your heart? Do you trust Him with everything?

_____

_____

_____

2. Are you fully submitted to the Lord?

_____

_____

_____

3. What is keeping you from fully submitting to God?

_____

_____

_____

_____

4. What do you need God to make clear concerning your life?

_____

_____

_____

_____

Day 37-

Ephesians 6:16
"In addition to all this, take up the shield of faith with which you can extinguish all the flaming arrows of the evil one."

Some days when you wake up and begin your day it oftentimes feels as though the devil is fighting you on every side. When it rains, it pours. If it's not one thing then it's another. You can't catch a break. Things never seem to work out. By noon you feel like you have gone through a 24-hour day already based on everything that you have had to fight through. It is very clear to me that the enemy loves to kill, steal, destroy and make our lives miserable. It also appears at times that there is absolutely nothing that we can do to stop his activity in our lives, but I am so glad that this isn't true.

The Bible teaches us that we have something we can use to fight back. We don't have to keep getting punched in the face, getting knocked down, and then lose after a ten count. The Bible says that we can take the shield of faith, which literally blocks the fiery darts of the enemy. It's your faith that you use to block what the enemy is trying to do in your life. When he throws something your way, the faith that you have in God will combat the attacks of the enemy. It may not seem like much, but faith in any believer's hand is really all you need.

My encouragement for you today is to strengthen and deepen your faith in God so that you can stand instead of being knocked down.

Be blessed!

Reflection Questions

1. What areas of your life do you need more faith in?

2. What areas of your life do you seem to be losing and not winning in?

3. Do you feel as though the devil is beating you up more than you are blocking his punches? Why?

4. What has stretched your faith in the past?

Day 38

Psalm 34:17
"The righteous cry out, and the Lord hears them; He
delivers them from all their troubles."

When I was younger I would get in a fair share of trouble. I don't think I was a bad child, but I would say that I was a bit mischievous. There were times when it seemed as though every day I found myself in some kind of trouble or some type of difficult situation. Being in trouble restricted me from going out, having fun, and doing what brought me joy. If you grew up in a home like mine, sometimes the consequences for trouble landed me in difficult and troubling circumstances. I received something called, spankings. During this painful ordeal I would cry out for help and relief. No matter how hard I cried the pain wouldn't end until the allotted time was over. I can remember on many occasions when the unbearable experience ended I would still be in serious tears from what I had gone through. And surprising to me, my mother would always say, "Stop crying or I will give you something to cry about." I could never understand why she didn't realize that if she never spanked me I would have never started crying. My tears never provoked her to stop, it seemed as though my tears made the pain worse. However, in the realm of the kingdom, when you cry out to God, not only does He hear but He gets you out of trouble. He doesn't want you to stop crying, He desires for you to keep calling out to Him for as long as you live.

My encouragement for you today is to keep
crying out to God.

Be blessed!

Reflection Questions

1. When was the last time you cried out to God for a considerable amount of time?

2. When you cry out to God, what is it usually about?

3. Do you think something is wrong with you if you keep calling out to God—especially about the same thing?

4. Take at least 15 minutes to release whatever is on your heart and whatever is weighing you down.

Day 39-

Psalm 27:5
"For in the day of trouble He will keep me safe in His dwelling..."

This is one of my favorite texts of scripture because it suggests that there are definitely times in our lives when we NEED to get away. There will be times in everyone's life when the stress and pressures of life are so big that God has to say to Himself that you NEED to be hidden. God says that when trouble hits your life, He will hide you! I am suggesting that when trouble hits your life there is a place where God takes you that trouble cannot find you because you will be hidden! That should make you excited because if you are honest—you need to go and hide right now. There are some things that you need to hide from because they are causing major problems and issues in your life. And look where God is hiding you—in His pavilion. It's almost as if God is saying that He is taking you away from trouble and hiding you in His personal resort place. No one is at this resort except for you and Him. Oftentimes you spend a lot of time fighting about where God is taking you and I want to suggest that this is not a place you can afford to miss. Your personal peace and your mental sanity depend on you being taken to this hidden place. Why not ask Him to take you there today?

My encouragement for you today is to accept the fact that there is a secret place where you can go.

Be blessed!

Reflection Questions

1. Could you use at least a week's vacation right now? How come?

_____

_____

_____

_____

2. Have you ever felt God's protection in your life? When?

_____

_____

_____

_____

3. Do you regularly meet God in His secret place? If not, why?

_____

_____

_____

_____

4. Is spending time with God difficult for you? Why?

_____

_____

_____

_____

Day 40-

Philippians 4:19
"And my God will meet all your needs according to the
riches of His glory in Christ Jesus."

ecause you are a child of God, you will never be empty handed. Since it is the responsibility of your Father-God to take care of you He has promised that you will never be without whatever He thinks you need. I know there are times in your life when you feel that you don't have enough or believe that you need a lot more to function. However, when you look back over your life, as difficult as some moments in your life have been God has always been looking out for you. This is critical because sometimes people take care of us because of what it can do for them. But the Word promises us that the way God cares for us is quite unlike anyone else. His concern is with supplying all of your needs.

Think about that...you have an endless supply of all your needs being met! God never runs out of resources to meet your needs, and he meets them according to His riches in glory in Christ Jesus. He meets and supplies your needs from His personal bank account that NEVER runs out. And if He never runs out, neither will you!

My encouragement for you today is to trust and
rest in the fact that every time God supplies one
of your needs His resources don't diminish just
because you received part of His riches.

Be blessed!

Reflection Questions

1. How many needs would you say you have? Name them.

2. Do you feel that you have been busy trying to take care of all of your needs?

3. Do you believe that God has an endless supply of resources?

4. Are you encouraged by how much God loves to take care of you?

About the Author

Noah Washington is an ordained pastor of the Seventh-day Adventist Church. He is extremely passionate about people discovering their Godly purpose. He and his wife Twila, have two children, Noah Alexander and Drew Mackenzie. In his leisure time, he enjoys listening to music, sports, and enjoying a good laugh.

Email/ pastornwash@gmail.com

Twitter/ @noahwash.me

Facebook/ Noah Washington

Instagram/ @noah_wash

noahwashington
Inspiring Purpose

Made in the USA
Middletown, DE
04 September 2023

37635185R00049